Cambridge Eng
June 2002

FANNY BURNEY

FANNY BURNEY

THE MOTHER OF ENGLISH FICTION

NIGEL NICOLSON

✳ SHORT BOOKS

First published in 2002 by
Short Books
15 Highbury Terrace
London N5 1UP

10 9 8 7 6 5 4 3 2 1

A CIP catalogue record for this book
is available from the British Library.

ISBN 1-904095-18-6

Printed in Great Britain by
Bookmarque Ltd, Croydon, Surrey

To Kathy Hill-Miller

Fanny Burney, painted by her cousin
Edward Francesco Burney in 1784

I

In the National Portrait Gallery in London you will find in the room devoted to 18th-century intellectuals two portraits, one above the other, a father and his daughter. The father is Dr Charles Burney, the composer and historian of music. His daughter is Frances, whom he and all her family and friends called Fanny. Fanny Burney she will remain here, despite the protests of some of her biographers, who have argued that the diminutive does less than justice to her achievement, as if Jane Austen were known to us as Jenny, the name by which her father called her at her birth.

In the portrait we see a young woman in a preposterous hat. The date is 1784, and she is 32 years old. The artist, her cousin Edward Francesco Burney, was half in love with her and she, aware of his infatuation, considered that he had flattered her, as in his other portrait of her, now at Parham Park, Sussex, in another huge hat, which he had painted two years earlier. She never claimed to be pretty, and was so 'near to being nothing', said a contemporary when Fanny was 27, 'that a gust of wind would blow her away'. She had a questing nose and a Gioconda smile, and was so short-sighted that she did not easily recognise people and when reading held the page close to her eyes. It is hard to believe from her demeanour in this portrait, her lack of conceit, her downward glance, that she was already one of the most famous women in England. She had published the first two of her novels, *Evelina* and *Cecilia*, and was the toast of Dr Johnson's circle. We can add to Edward's painting characteristics that he was not skilled enough to convey – her intelligence, wit and mischief; qualities not inconsistent with those that he does express – her modesty and gentleness. She was a lovable woman, more anxious to please by her cleverness than to wound.

The other picture in the National Portrait Gallery, of her father, is a masterpiece. It is by his friend, Sir Joshua Reynolds. Charles Burney is 55. He had recently been made a Doctor of Music and was determined that the world should know it. He wears the full robes of his doctorate and grasps a rolled-up musical score like a field marshal's baton. His features are very pleasing. He has an impish smile – sardonic, provocative, amused – and one can sympathise with Doctor Johnson's tributes to him, 'that clever dog Burney', and 'I love Burney, my heart goes out to meet him'. Johnson was not a man to be taken in by an ambitious scamp. Burney had risen by his own talents from a humble music teacher to become a man of letters, the author of the famous four-volume *History of Music*, who could hold his own with the greatest wits of the day. The son of a feckless Scotsman, James MacBurney (Charles dropped the Mac because he considered it a handicap in England), he knew that the only way to succeed in a strictly layered society when you were penniless and unknown was by being amusing, smart and pleasing to ladies. You must not shrink from the guiles of flattery nor the shame of being patronised, and you must learn, learn, learn all the time, from observation, books and talk. Burney once said that he never went to bed without having learnt

Charles Burney

something he didn't know when he awoke, and if that is true of any newspaper reader, the difference is that Charles remembered it.

He was a pupil of the celebrated Dr Arne, the composer of 'Rule Britannia', and was engaged by Fulke Greville, a rich aristocrat, first as his harpsichordist, and then, delighting in his company, as a friend whom he was happy to introduce into high society. When he was 23, Charles married Esther Sleepe. Their daughter Esther (Hetty) was born a month before their wedding, a fact that Fanny was careful to suppress when she came to write her father's life. The elder Esther was an excellent woman of strong character, surpassing beauty, musically well educated and with a taste for literature. She had eight other children, of whom Fanny was the fourth, and Fanny adored her.

Charles Burney was still without a steady occupation. After leaving Greville he earned a precarious living as a music teacher, organist and composer of occasional pieces for the Drury Lane Theatre, but his health deteriorated (consumption was suspected) to such an extent that he was obliged to leave London for a more salubrious environment. He was offered the post of organist at King's Lynn, Norfolk, and much against his will, for it seemed to him like exile, he took the job at a salary of £100 a year. It was at King's Lynn that Fanny was born on 13 June 1752, and she spent the first eight years of her life there.

Lynn was not the backwater that Burney had feared. It was a bustling seaport with excellent municipal buildings of which a few survive, and it boasted a lively provincial society that immediately took to the young organist and his wife. He found that they were lamentably ignorant of music, and the organ at St Margaret's church was 'execrably bad', but he was soon won over by their friendliness. The leading citizens employed him to teach their daughters the piano, and from that beginning his clientele spread into the surrounding countryside. By his good-fellowship and love of the arts he won a welcome to the great Norfolk houses of Holkham, Houghton, Felbrigg and Blickling, as a guest, not tutor, when there were no daughters to teach.

Opinions differed about Fanny as a child. Her father thought her slow, the most backward of all his children, and she was known in the family as 'the little dunce'. But she was never morose. A schoolfriend remembered her as 'so merry, so gay, so droll and with such imagination for making plays, always something new, something of her own contrivance'. With strangers she was abnormally shy. They dubbed her 'the old lady'. Although she was the least musical of the Burney children, her love of literature expanded as soon as she could read. She taught herself French from Voltaire, Italian from Dante and Petrarch, and the classics in translation. Charles forbade her to read fiction except for Fielding's *Amelia* and improving moral tales. Her memory was excellent. She could repeat long passages from Shakespeare and Dryden after a first reading. The 'dunce' image soon fell away.

And she began to write. We know little of her earliest essays because she burned them. Nearly fifty years later, in the preface to her last novel *The Wanderer*, she explained that her motive was that she was ashamed of what she had written and feared discovery by her father, who disapproved of women's writing. 'On my fifteenth birthday,' she wrote,

I made so resolute a conquest over an inclination at which I blushed, and that I had always kept secret, that I committed to the flames whatever, up to that moment, I had committed to paper. And so enormous was the pile, that I thought it prudent to consume it in the garden.

Among the manuscripts which she destroyed was the draft of a novel, *Carolyne Evelyn*, and elegies, odes, tragedies and epic poems, of which only her favourite sister Susanna (Susan) knew the existence. But having caught the habit and discovered her gift, her resolution to write no more lasted barely six months. 'My bureau was closed, but my head was not emptied.' Her next venture was not fiction or poetry, but diary-letters, describing the events of the day and the characters of their visitors. She intended them for no other eyes but her own. They were addressed to 'nobody', the intimate who did not exist. Of course her industry was soon discovered, and a friend of the family, Dorothy Young, was deputed to tell Fanny to give it up. This was the scene, as Fanny described it in the diary:

She says that it is the most dangerous employment a young

person can have – it makes them often record things which ought not to be recorded. I told her that as my journal was solely for my own perusal, nobody could be displeased at my writing anything.

'But how can you answer,' said she, 'that it *is* only for your perusal? If any improper person finds it, you know not the uneasiness it may cost you… Suppose that anybody finds a part in which they are extremely censured?'

'Why, then, they must take it for their pains. It was not wrote for them but for me.'

'Suppose that you were to fall in love, and then the object of your passion were to get sight of some part which related to himself?'

'Why then, Miss Young, I must make a little trip to Rosamund's pond.' *

The Burneys had moved to London when Fanny's mother died prematurely, and she was succeeded by Charles's second wife, a wealthy widow from King's Lynn whom Fanny detested. It was she who urged Miss Young to remonstrate with her step-daughter. Fanny was only 16, determined not to be bullied by a

* Rosamund's pond, in St James's Park, was a favourite rendezvous for suicides.

17

prude into abandoning what she regarded partly as an amusement, and more seriously as a literary exercise. She was teaching herself to observe, to remember, to record, and quickly developed a style, highly original for its detail and veracity, particularly in reproducing conversations. She used colloquialisms, slang, sentences broken off, words wrongly used, some invented, like 'dabble', 'skipping-rope', 'lunch-party' and 'elbow' as a verb, words that originated with her and passed into the language. She was adept at reproducing people's facial and body language, by which they betrayed what they were thinking but not saying, and how relations between the sexes, different age groups, family members and acquaintances were affected by minor incidents, chance conversations and significant silences. If we allow that she might sometimes burnish a person's remarks if she admired them, or render them more absurd if she disliked them, her recollection always bore the stamp of authenticity. We discover what people were like, how they talked and moved. They are not caricatures.

Her mother's death had shaken her dreadfully.

Though it is scarcely believable, it indicates the depth of her despair that she read through the entire Bible – from Genesis to Revelations – three times to console herself. Then the excitement of London life, and a particular friendship, revived her spirits and stimulated her literary ambition. The friend was an elderly man, Samuel Crisp. He had been her father's friend who had believed in him enough to persuade him to leave King's Lynn, where his talents, Crisp considered, were in danger of becoming atrophied. Crisp himself was a cultured man, widely read and travelled, a dilettante with a good singing voice. He had failed as a playwright, and retreated to his country house, Chessington in Surrey, a rambling old house up a muddy track, where his main amusement was in cultivating Fanny Burney. Her private journals became letters to 'my dear Daddy', as she called him, and she never hesitated to tell him what she would not even tell her sisters. Crisp nursed her like a hot-house plant. She was 'my Fannikin', who gave him, as young women often do to men old enough for the innocence of their relationship to be beyond suspicion, a new interest in his lonely life. He understood what she was attempting as a writer. He told her to enjoy the surge and spray of the spoken language, and avoid losing its vitality in prose. 'I hate it,' he wrote to her, 'if you sit about framing studied letters, that are to be correct, nicely grammatical and run in smooth periods. The sudden sallies of imagination, clap'd down on paper, just as they arise, are worth Folios.'

Fanny would describe for him the visit of James Bruce, the Scottish explorer, who returned to London claiming, falsely, that he had discovered the source of the Nile, a bull of a man in appearance and manner; or David Garrick, the actor who, finding Charles Burney away from home, cried to the girls, 'Here ye all are – one two, three, four – beauties all,' and for half an hour entertained them with mimicry and pantomime, ending by flinging himself into an armchair, exhausted. This was the world that Burney had created for his family, for though he was still poor, earning a precarious living by teaching music, he attracted to his house in Poland Street, Soho, then to the one in Queen's Square, Bloomsbury, and finally to the house in St Martin's Street, off Leicester Square (a house that had once belonged to Isaac Newton) the most invigorating society of the day – Boswell, Joshua Reynolds, Edmund Burke, Garrick, Samuel Johnson, Robert Adam, Christopher Smart the poet, and Italian castrati to sing to them. Macaulay wrote of these entertainments, 'He belonged in fortune and station to the middle class. Yet few nobles could assemble in the most stately mansions a society so various and brilliant as was sometimes to be found in Dr. Burney's cabin.' Fanny kept quiet in their company. She was still shy, even prudish, nervous of being seen not fully dressed, unwilling to consider even the idea of a lover for herself while mocking her sisters' admirers, and deeply resentful that men should regard women as decorative playthings. On returning from a wedding she reflected, 'How short a time does it take to put an eternal end to a woman's liberty.' She was determined to use her pen to protest against the vulnerability of people like herself, and she would shape her protest in the form of a novel. At the age of 24 she began to write *Evelina*.

II

The seeds of the book can be traced much earlier, in her letters and diaries, and possibly in her destroyed novel *Carolyne Evelyn*. She felt obliged to conceal her writing from her father, who made his own literary demands on her by having her copy the manuscript of his vast *History of Music*. *Evelina* is the story of a girl who has been brought up in seclusion by a guardian, the Reverend Villars, an elderly Dorset clergyman not unlike Samuel Crisp, and who is sent by him to London, to further her education and be introduced into society. She is beautiful and clever and falls in love with the handsome Lord Orville, whom, after many disappointments and escapades, she marries. The shape of the novel is epistolary, an exchange of letters mainly between Mr Villars, admonitory, and Evelina, girlish, alternately excited by the glamour of the metropolis and horrified by its vulgarity. But Evelina, like Fanny, is no sop. She earns the respect of insolent men by her intelligence and self-reliance. Her disapproval of their licentiousness is never priggish. It is shot through by her sense of the ridiculous, and her gift, which she shared with her creator, for investing comedy with a serious moral message. Innocence is abused, but is always in the end triumphant. Fanny was capable, as Jane Austen, who much admired the book, never was, of depicting dreadful scenes of inhumanity, as when a pair of fops set two poor old women to race each other for a bet, and she could draw depraved characters like Evelina's grandmother in these brutal terms:

> Her head-dress had fallen off; her linen was torn; her negligée had not a pin left in it; her petticoats she was obliged to hold on; and her shoes were perpetually slipping off. She was covered with dirt, weeds, and filth, and her face was really horrible, for the pomatum and powder from her head, and the dust from the road, were quite pasted on her skin by her tears, which, with her rouge, made so frightful a mixture that she hardly looked human.

Was it this sort of passage that induced Virginia

Woolf to call Fanny Burney the 'Mother of English Fiction'?

The novel owes much to her sense of drama. It is rich in incident, and much of the narrative is carried forward by dialogue. In her letters to Crisp, she had long practised the same techniques, and as she intended to publish the book anonymously, she was uninhibited in making use of her own experience. It is partly autobiographical: Evelina is the girl Fanny wished she was.

She was anxious, above all, not to distress her father, and was so determined to conceal her authorship from him that she made a copy of her manuscript in a disguised hand, in case he should find it. Her fear was that she might bring disrepute on him and her family for her satire on the many people whom they knew, and for her knowledge of the corruption of urban life of which respectable young women were supposed to be ignorant. Longing for publication, she adopted a device which would achieve it without giving herself away. She persuaded her brother Charles, heavily disguised as a Mr King, to take the manuscript of the first two volumes to a bookseller-printer, Thomas Lowndes of Fleet

Street, requesting him to send his reply to a coffee shop in the Haymarket, where it would be collected. Lowndes reacted favourably, but insisted, before he could make up his mind, on seeing the third volume, which Fanny had not yet written. Working feverishly, mostly at night, away from her father's scrutiny, she completed it, and Lowndes accepted the whole work with alacrity.

Unwilling to deceive her father totally, Fanny remarked, casually, that she was 'writing a book'. Unsuspecting, Dr Burney laughed, calling her his rival author, but did not enquire what the book was about, and then forgot it. Lowndes rushed out a first edition in January 1778. Fanny had sold him the copyright for thirty guineas, which seemed to her 'an enormous sum', and never made another penny by it.

Evelina was an instant success. The critics were adulatory, the influential *Monthly Review* saying, 'We do not hesitate to pronounce it one of the most sprightly, entertaining and agreeable productions of this kind which has of late fallen under our notice.' The first edition soon sold out. Others were hastily printed. Everyone was guessing the author's identity. Lowndes himself thought it must be by a man, perhaps Horace Walpole. Sir Joshua Reynolds said that he would give £50 to know the author, little realising that he already knew her. Fanny knew that the truth must soon leak out. Her siblings already knew it, and very carefully she allowed it to become known to the two people whose opinion she most valued – Samuel Crisp and her father. She teased Crisp, who had read the book, that her father had divulged to her the name of the author and she invited him to guess:

'I can't guess,' said he, 'Maybe it's you?' Oddso, thought I, what do you mean by that? 'Pho, nonsense!' cried I, 'What should make you think of me?' 'Why, you look guilty,' answered he.

She kept him in ignorance a few weeks longer. To her father the revelation was more delicate. He had read the book without suspicion, but did not know the truth until five months after publication. Then Susan told him. The significance of the dedication, 'To -----, oh author of my being! far more dear to me than light', flashed over him. He rushed down to Chessington, embraced her, and said, 'Fanny, I have read your book – but you need not blush at it – it is full of merit – it is, really, extraordinary!' She sobbed on his shoulder with relief.

Charles Burney stifled whatever scruples he may at first have felt when he became aware that *Evelina*, whose authorship was now becoming widely known, was universally praised, and that Fanny, aged 25, had acquired the fame for which he had manoeuvred for so long. He would gain by it vicariously. The judgment that he was most anxious to hear was that of Dr Johnson and Mrs Thrale, in whose house at Streatham the Doctor had taken up almost permanent residence, to the annoyance of Mr Thrale. Burney had taught music to their daughter Queenie. He need not have worried. Johnson, after reading the first volume, demanded the second and third. 'There are passages in it', he said, 'which might do honour to Richardson,' and then he asked to meet Fanny, who came, quaking, to Streatham, where she saw a copy of the book lying prominently on the drawing-room table. 'I hid it under other books, for

I should die – or faint at least – if anybody was to pick it up, innocently, while I am here.' Johnson, aged 68, treated her with great kindness. He praised her book for its understanding of human nature, which contrasted so unexpectedly with her shy demeanour. Mrs Thrale asked her how she could possibly know so much about human vice, and she was at a loss for an answer. Johnson petted her, embraced her tenderly, called her 'My little Burney', 'My dear love', 'Oh you little character-monger, you!'. She gradually grew less shy of him, but avoided profound discussion for fear that he would discover her lack of sophistication. She thought 'his face the most ugly, his person the most awkward, and his manners the most singular that ever were', but their friendship grew so rapidly that he would reproach her for neglecting him when she was constantly at his side.

Mrs Thrale responded to her with equal warmth, even to the extent of giving money to her father, who scrupled not to receive it. Fanny came to adore her, describing her as 'a most dear creature, but never restrains her tongue in anything; nor indeed any of her feelings – she laughs, cries, scolds, sports, reasons, makes fun – does everything she has an inclination to do without any study of prudence or thought of blame.' They drew so close that Mrs Thrale invited her to spend weeks on end at Streatham, took her to her other house in Brighton and on a long visit to Bath, where Fanny was treated as a celebrity, refusing to dance on the only occasion when they visited the Assembly Rooms for fear of being pointed out by strangers. She hated the fame for which she had so much longed, detesting compliments of the kind that she quoted in a letter to Susan, 'Oh miss, you deserve everything. You wrote the best and prettiest book!'

Crisp urged her to write a play, and so did Sheridan, seeing in her novel a potential dramatist, and after recoiling from the suggestion because she thought it wrong to display on the stage evil characters who should only appear in print, she wrote *The Witlings*, a comedy of manners which opens in a milliner's shop. It was an utter failure, never performed, and condemned even by Crisp, but unfairly, because it is a lively, original piece. Her father forbade her to put it on the stage, possibly for fear of offending ladies of his acquaintance who might consider themselves caricatured in it. Its failure was a terrible shock to Fanny, who secretly fancied herself more as a dramatist than a novelist. *The Witlings* was not even published until 1995, from the single manuscript that survives in the Berg Collection, New York.

Following this disaster, and anxious as much for his own sake as for hers to retrieve her reputation and earning power, Dr Burney urged her to write another novel. She wrote *Cecilia*. It was twice as long as *Evelina*, over 1,000 pages in print, and it took her three years to write. Nothing of her gift for comedy had faded, but the book was more sophisticated than its predecessor, less liable to descend into farce. It was the story of another girl, Cecilia Beverley, beautiful and clever, who had inherited a fortune on condition that her future husband, whoever he might be, took her name on marriage. Pending that event, Cecilia lived with her guardian, Compton Delvile, with whose son Mortimer she fell deeply in love. They could marry only if he became Mortimer Beverley, a proposition which his snobbish father furiously refused to entertain, or if Cecilia renounced her fortune, which she and her lover were quite prepared to do. Their plan was defeated by an intriguing, disreputable man called Monckton who had married a rich dowager forty years older than himself, and hoped, when his wife died, to marry Cecilia himself and collar her fortune. Cecilia saw through his duplicity, and married her Mortimer without forfeiting her money or he his name, and old Delvile was eventually reconciled to the match.

In *Cecilia* Fanny Burney abandoned the epistolary pattern of her first novel for straight narrative. It is a muscular book, taut with conflict, and dwells on what became a central theme in all her books, the injustice of the class system, which obliged the poor to struggle for self-respect and encouraged the rich to ignore their misery, even refusing to pay the bills of their 'insolent' creditors. Much of the detail was drawn from Fanny's experience of Brighton and Bath, and Mrs Delvile is a close portrait of Mrs Thrale.

A second novel is often scorched by the critics as a poor successor to the first. Not so *Cecilia*: it enjoyed an even greater success. Mrs Thrale said, 'Nothing was ever so entertaining, so seducing, so delightful,' and

Dr Johnson so much admired it that he told Fanny, 'We shall go down hand-in-hand to posterity.' Queen Charlotte read it at Windsor. Gibbon claimed to have read it in a day. 'Impossible', said Burke. 'It cost me three days, and you know I never parted with it from the time I opened it.' Charles Burney boasted of his daughter's renewed success. Although Fanny's name was not on the title page ('by the author of *Evelina*'), everyone who mattered discovered it from him or his friends. This time Fanny made a little more money, £250 for a first edition of 2,000 copies but nothing more.

Then three events occurred that profoundly altered Fanny's life. Samuel Crisp ('that all but matchless man') died in 1783; Mrs Thrale, now a widow, married Gabriel Piozzi; and Fanny, for the first time, fell in love.

Piozzi was a poor Italian music teacher, and when both were aged 40, Hester Thrale, now widowed, determined to marry him. Her daughter Queenie, Dr Johnson and all their friends, including Fanny Burney, were horrified. Johnson, who died three months after the marriage, told Fanny, 'I desire never to hear of her more,' and burned every letter of hers in his possession.

Fanny, who considered that Mrs Thrale was 'duped by ungovernable passion', wrote to her directly, 'Children, religion, friends, country and character, all is at stake – and for what? – a gratification that no man can esteem, not even he for whom you feel it.' No friendship could survive so great an insult. So within a few months Fanny lost her three closest friends, Crisp, Johnson and Thrale. The marriage turned out much more happily than they foretold. Piozzi was a musician, teacher and singer of considerable talent. He had no money, but that was no obstacle to their happiness since Hester let the Streatham house profitably and sold her first husband's brewery business for £135,000. They lived in mutual esteem until Piozzi's death in 1809. In a way, he was a more satisfactory husband for her than Henry Thrale who had not shared her intellectual and social gifts.

Fanny's unreciprocated love was for a clergyman, George Owen Cambridge, who was younger than her by four years. He was a friend of Molesworth Phillips, Susan's husband, and in every way could have made for her a perfect partner – handsome, intelligent, pleasant in manner and modest. She was first attracted to him by his refusal to flatter her, not even mentioning her novels. As rumour spread that she was in love with him, she affected indifference, but her journals are full of him, and she read into his most trivial remarks ('Oh I am so glad you spoke to me!') far more than he intended. She wrote that she was 'passive', meaning that she was awaiting the move he never made. Then with the resignation of young women cheated of love and denied by convention the right to express it, she took refuge in submission: 'If he wishes to shun me, he surely knows why, and I am the last person in the world to willingly defeat his purpose.' That is what she wrote, but it was not what she felt. In her next novel, *Camilla*, she reflected: 'Since Man must choose Woman, or Woman Man, which should come forward to make the choice? Which should retire to be chosen?'

III

Then something happened to Fanny Burney which Crisp, had he lived, would certainly have tried to prevent. For five years, 1786-91, she became Second Keeper of the Robes to Queen Charlotte, wife of George III. It came about not through her own wish, for she was appalled by the prospect, but owing to the social ambition of her father. He had dedicated his *History of Music* to the Queen, and had applied without success for the post of Master of the King's Band. His chief sponsor for the job had been Mary Delany, a widow aged over 80, who was universally loved and admired for her wit and an art form that she had perfected, a collage of differently coloured papers which she cut with amazing dexterity into the shapes of leaves and flowers. The King, who shared her love of botany, gave her a pension of £200 a year and a grace-and-favour house at Windsor, where he was a frequent visitor. It was there that Fanny first met the King, and the conversation that followed is one of the most famous in her journals. He asked Mrs Delany:

'Pray, does Miss Burney draw too?' The *too* was pronounced very civilly.

'I believe not, sir,' answered Mrs Delany, 'at least she does not tell.'

'Oh!', cried he, laughing 'that's nothing! She is not apt to tell, she never does tell, you know! Her father told me that himself. He told me the whole history of her *Evelina*. And I shall never forget his face when he spoke of his feelings at first taking up the book! – he looked quite frightened, just as if he was doing it that moment!'

Then coming up close to me he said, 'But what? – what? – how was it?'

'Sir', cried I, not well understanding him.

'How came you – how happened it – what? – what?'

'I – I only wrote, sir, for my own amusement – only in some odd, idle hours.'

'But your publishing – your printing – how was that?'

'That was only, sir – only because... I thought, sir, it would look very well in print!'

I do really flatter myself this is the silliest speech I ever made! I am quite provoked with myself for it, but a fear of laughing made me eager to utter anything. He laughed very heartily himself – well he might – and walked away to enjoy it, crying out, 'Very fair, indeed! That's being very fair and honest!'

At that chance interview there was no suggestion that Fanny should join the Court, but Mrs Delany pressed her claims, supported strongly by Dr Burney, without either of them believing it possible that Fanny might wish to refuse. She thought the appointment more of a humiliation than an honour, and accepted it only for her father's sake, hoping that if George Cambridge would bring himself to propose to her, marriage would give her a means of escape. He did not propose, and she took up her duties at Windsor in July 1786. She was given a pleasant apartment outside the Castle, a maid and footman to attend her and £200 a year. Her duties were to dress the Queen twice a day (but only her outer garments), and to amuse her. Fanny had little interest in clothes, and so untrained was she in hairdressing that the Queen shrieked aloud when Fanny tied her bow inside instead of outside her hair. For the rest of the day she had to sit in her room in case the Queen rang for her. She was allowed no holidays, and no visitors except by express permission. The royal couple were not unkind to her, but she never knew when she could behave towards them with her natural friendliness, for, as in all Courts, formality and good humour were mixed in variable proportions. For instance, Fanny was never permitted to sit in the Queen's presence, even when she was reading a book aloud to her, and on leaving her, she must take her first steps backwards. The King showed his affection for her more openly. He allowed her to share with him Herschel's telescope to look at Saturn's rings, and it was to her that he uttered his famous remark about Shakespeare:

'Was there ever,' cried he, 'such stuff as great part of Shakespeare? Only one must not say so! But what think you – what? – is there not sad stuff? What? What?'

'Yes, indeed I think so, sir, though mixed with such excellencies that –'

'Oh!,' cried he, laughing good-humouredly, 'I know it is not well to be said! But it's true. Only it's Shakespeare, and nobody dare abuse him.'

On another occasion he asked her, 'How goes the Muse?', without realising that of all trades writing is the most private. The truth was that the Muse was not going well at all. In her five years at Court, Fanny wrote only two unfinished tragedies. It might have occurred to her that she could write the most popular novel of all time – about *them* – but she desisted, even after her retirement from the Court, and confined her observations to her diary and letters to her sisters. In them, she of course exaggerated the etiquette to make a better story. She wrote to Hetty:

In the first place, you must not cough. If you find a cough tickling in your throat, you must arrest it from making any sound. In the second place, you must not sneeze. If a sneeze still insists upon working its way, you must oppose it, by keeping your teeth grinding together. In the third place, you must not stir either hand or foot. If, by chance, a black pin runs into your head, you must not take it out. You may privately bite the inside of your cheek, and if you gnaw a piece out, be sure either to swallow it or commit it to a corner of your mouth till they are gone – for you must not spit.

Her greatest relief was to talk and play with the Princesses, and her greatest trial was Mrs Schwellenberg, Fanny's superior and a favourite of the Queen who had brought her from Germany on her marriage. She was a cross, selfish woman who spoke English with difficulty, and was jealous of Fanny, who hated her. One day Mrs Schwellenberg told her that the Queen had decided to give Fanny a gown, adding with a sneer, 'The Queen says that you are not rich.' Fanny, humiliated, said that she didn't need a gown, as she had two already. Mrs Schwellenberg took offence at this: 'Miss Bernar, I tell you at once, when the Queen will give you a gown, you must be humble, thankful.' She was obliged to accept it, and wore it on the Princess Royal's birthday, when the King called out, 'You should see Miss Burney's gown now, and she would think her fine enough!' The King's manner, before he lost his reason, enchanted her. He would ride in Windsor Great

Park without any escort, chatting with rustics who had no idea who he was. Within the palace he would wander around in search of company, knocking on the equerry's door at 5 am, or accosting Fanny in the corridors, where she was supposed to flatten herself against the wall at his approach, and ask her to join him in a cup of tea. Her resentment at being imprisoned in a gilded cage was tempered by his kindness.

She had diversions. She continued to see much of Mrs Delany and helped her write her memoirs, but when the old lady died in April 1788, Fanny was thrown back for society on the Court. Her choice of companions was not too stodgy. There was a succession of handsome ADCs and attractive ladies-in-waiting, and Fanny fell half in love with the Queen's vice-chamberlain, Stephen Digby, a 46-year-old widower with four children. An ex-soldier, he was a charming man, given to melancholy, but interested in literature and the arts. With the King he had exceptional influence, of which Fanny recorded an example. In the middle of the night the King rose from his bed in a state of agitation and Digby found him wandering along the corridors. He went boldly up to him, took him by the arm and begged him to go back to bed. 'Who are you?' asked the King indignantly. 'I am Mr Digby, sir,' he replied, 'and your Majesty has been very good to me often. Now I am going to be very good to you, for you must come to bed, sir; it is necessary for your life.' It was this gentle, steadfast man with whom Fanny imagined herself to be in love, and him with her. He had shown her marked attention, often visiting her room when he had no other motive than to enjoy her company. When she heard that he was engaged to marry one of the maids of honour, Charlotte Gunning, she could scarcely believe it. 'He has committed a breach of all moral ties,' she confided to her journal. He had certainly never asked her to marry him, but 'honourably and morally' he should have given her the right of refusal. She would not have exercised that right. She would have accepted him, if not for love, as a means of escaping from the Court. It was a repetition of the George Cambridge affair, but even more bruising to her pride.

Fanny was not confined to Windsor. She followed the Court to Kew and Richmond, accompanied the monarch on his provincial tours, and was allowed by him to attend non-royal functions such as the trial of Warren Hastings in Westminster Hall, where she heard Burke, Fox and Sheridan speak for the prosecution and Hastings in his own defence, all of which she recounted to the King and Queen, delighting them with the fidelity and detail of her narrative. She had become, inadvertently, the court jester and storyteller. One incident, when George III's wits had temporarily deserted him, illustrates her hold on his affections. She was walking in Kew Gardens, when, to her surprise, she saw the King and two of his doctors coming towards her. She turned and ran, only to hear herself pursued by the King, calling out 'Miss Burney! Miss Burney!':

I protest I was ready to die. I knew not in what state he might be. On I ran, too terrified to stop but still the poor hoarse voice rang in my ears – the attendants all running to catch their eager master… When they were within a few yards of me, the King called out, 'Why did you run away?' Shocked at a question impossible to answer, yet a little assured by the mild tone of his voice, I instantly forced myself forward to meet him and met all his wonted benignity of countenance, though something still of wildness in his eyes. Think, however, of my surprise, to feel him put his hands round my two shoulders, and then kiss my cheek... He then spoke of Mrs Schwellenberg, laughing, and saying, 'Never mind her! Don't be oppressed – I am your friend' and kissed me again.

When the Court went on a west-country tour in 1789, the welcome of the crowds was heightened by contrast with contemporary events in France, where Louis XVI was a virtual prisoner of the revolutionaries. At Weymouth, girls scattered flowers under the wheels of the royal carriage and bands accompanied the King's dips into the sea. Near Plymouth, they stayed at Saltram House, recently decorated and furnished by Robert Adam, Chippendale, Wedgwood and Joshua Reynolds, and Fanny, still hoping for an offer from Stephen Digby, noticed how carefully he prepared a slice of brown bread for her, but on another occasion drew his chair away from her when he sat down.

She became increasingly unhappy. It was not only Digby's defection that distressed her, but the ritual of the Court, her loss of privacy and freedom, the wearisome duties that separated her from her true friends. Horace Walpole asked her, 'Are your talents to be buried in obscurity?' and Boswell, who met her by chance in St. George's Chapel, Windsor, said to her, 'I am extremely glad to see you, but very sorry to see you here. My dear ma'am, why do you stay? It won't do: you must resign,' and he offered to organise a petition to Dr. Burney to remove her. Eventually, in July 1791, she did resign. The Queen reluctantly accepted her decision and promised her a pension of £100 a year. Her farewell to the King was more emotional:

He advanced to the window, where I stood, to speak to me. I was not then able to comport myself steadily. I was forced to turn my head away from him. He stood still and silent for some minutes, waiting to see if I should turn about, but I could not recover myself sufficiently to face him, and perceiving me quite overcome, he walked away, and I saw him no more.

She had served the Crown for five years, all but ten days, and was now at liberty.

IV

Fanny returned to London and shared a room with her half-sister at Chelsea College, where her father had the post of organist. She had no employment, wrote nothing, and hung fire until her life was transformed by the most unexpected of the many twists that shaped it. At the age of 40, she married a penniless French émigré, Alexandre d'Arblay.

It came about like this. A group of French aristocrats, soldiers and statesmen, exiled by the Revolution, took refuge in England, where one of them, Madame de Staël, rented a large country house in Surrey, Juniper Hall, where they could stay until their fortunes turned. They had no notion what the future held for them, for they were welcome neither in France because they had supported the monarchy, nor in England because they had argued for limiting the monarch's power. It was said that they had precipitated the Revolution by advocating change and, from ignorance, xenophobia and prejudice, the British regarded them not as victims of the Revolution, but as its perpetrators. When the King was guillotined, and their distress led them almost to renounce their nationality, they were held responsible for his murder. At Juniper Hall they lived in unaccustomed simplicity, and endlessly discussed their fate.

Surrey did not take kindly to these cuckoos thrust into its nest. The local gentry were fascinated by their presence but scandalised by their politics and morals, and the Juniper group, few of whom spoke adequate English, had little inducement to seek their company. There were two exceptions. They were warmly welcomed by the Lock family of nearby Norbury Hall, and at a cottage in the village of Mickleham, not half a mile from Juniper, which belonged to Fanny's beloved sister Susan and her husband, Captain Molesworth Phillips. It was Susan, who spoke excellent French, having been partly educated in Paris, who first befriended the colony, and wrote endless letters to her sister describing them.

Among the leading figures were the Charles de

Talleyrand, Comte and Comtesse de Châtre, Comte Louis de Narbonne, Alexandre d'Arblay and Mme. Germaine de Staël. Susan was greatly excited by them, particularly by Narbonne, d'Arblay and de Staël. Narbonne had been temporarily Minister of War in Paris, a position from which he was dismissed in 1791. For three years he was de Staël's lover and she had a child by him. By her marriage to the Swedish Ambassador to France, a feeble, querulous, lascivious man for whom she felt no affection, she gained diplomatic immunity, and used her position to assist the escape of her lover to England. Following the birth of their child in Switzerland, she managed to join him at Juniper Hall in January 1793, six days after Louis XVI's execution. She brought with her a welcome sum of money and her acute intelligence. She was only 26, deficient in good looks, but celebrated for her scintillating conversational gifts. A contemporary said of her, 'One is swept away by the force of her genius. When she is present, other people just become the audience.' Fanny compared her to Mrs Thrale: 'They had the same sort of highly superior intellect, the same depth of learning, the same buoyant animal spirits, such as neither sickness, sorrow or even terror could subdue.'

When Fanny first met the group at Norbury Park, she wrote to her father, 'There could be nothing imagined more charming, more fascinating than this colony,' and on meeting Talleyrand for the first time, 'It is inconceivable what a convert he has made of me. His powers of entertainment are astonishing, both in information and raillery.' Her intimacy with Germaine de Staël grew rapidly. Each admired the other's books, and Fanny was intoxicated by her society, which was all the more remarkable because she did not trust herself to speak French correctly and the brilliance of de Staël's conversation must have made her formidable in company. When Jane Austen was invited to meet her ten years later, she refused, fearing not so much the competition as the glare of her personality. Fanny was at first ignorant of her infidelity with Narbonne, and when she was told of it, she was deeply shocked. She declared to her father that it could not be true, and indeed, to de Staël's distress, it was already weakened by Narbonne's liaisons with other women, notably Mlle

Louise de Contat of the Comédie Française. To test him, Germaine asked him, 'Suppose that Mlle Contat and I were both about to drown, which of us would you save first?' 'Madame', he replied, 'I am convinced that you are an excellent swimmer.'

Alexandre d'Arblay was 38 in 1792. A soldier by profession, he had been adjutant general to Lafayette, the French hero of the American War of Independence. When the Revolution broke out, he was stripped of his commission and all his possessions and took refuge in Holland, from where Narbonne, his intimate friend, brought him to Juniper Hall. His character was not unlike Samuel Crisp's, for 'its openness, probity, intellectual knowledge and unhackneyed manners', as Fanny described him. In his unpractical, optimistic way he gave little thought to his future and considered it no disgrace to be dependent on de Staël's charity. He was a naturally happy man, filled with animal spirits, but contemplative and studious too, seldom without a book in his hands when he was not joining eagerly in conversation. Fanny began by offering to teach him English if he would teach her better French, and their intimacy grew

Alexandre d'Arblay

in the exchange of *thèmes* in the other's language, which each would correct before returning it. By imperceptible steps the *thèmes* grew into missives of mutual affection. Fanny sent copies of them to Susan, as well as writing to her almost daily accounts of what she began to recognise as d'Arblay's courtship. I have sat in the Berg Collection of New York Public Library reading some of them, and I noted how artless they were, written without correction, and how much she was enjoying the drama of his hesitant moves towards her and her maidenly responses, never provocative but never discouraging. Once he appeared at Chelsea College, having walked most of the way from Juniper Hall, carrying a rose tree, which he left for her with a note. She thought it must be from Norbury Park,

> but I was not very placid and composed when I saw the note was from M. d'Arblay. My father immediately asked if it was Mrs Lock's hand – and I concluded all now would follow. I felt almost ready to die. I was forced to answer, 'No sir, t'is a *thème*, I believe from M. d'Arblay.'

D'Arblay knew that Dr Burney would look upon his

courtship with disapproval, because he had no money and no hope in England of earning any, and because he was a Catholic by religion and one of a political group which had weakened the French monarchy. D'Arblay's nervousness sometimes seemed to Fanny like the gibbering of an ape, and she did not hesitate to reproduce for Susan examples of it:

He hid his face upon my hand, which he would not suffer me to loosen. I felt half gasping with apprehension at what was to follow.

'*C'est – c'est que – puisque vous ne voulez pas que je vous parle –*'

'O no! no! no!' I cried.

'*Eh bien – puisque vous ne me permettez pas – puisque vous me défendez de vous parler – puisque, absolument, vous –*'

I repeated my negative warmly.

'*Eh bien, donc – permettez, au moins – que je parle – à quelque autre! – à une – que vous aimez bien!*'

O how I was out of breath at this request. I said not a word.

'*à – à – enfin – à Madame Phillips?*'

So Susan herself was to be the intermediary. When Fanny told her sister that she wished for his sake that she was younger and prettier, Susan replied, 'No matter! But you should wish yourself *richer*!', for in truth they would have nothing to live on other than Fanny's pension of £100 from the Crown, which the Queen might withdraw if she married a man who might be regarded at Windsor as a regicide. Fanny, by this time desperately in love, argued that they could live very simply. Curates had lived on less. She could write another book. William Lock supported her, but Narbonne ridiculed the idea.

'Even if the pension is honoured,' he said to Susan, 'they will have to live like peasants. And how will Miss Burney feel when she finds herself the subject of a thousand impertinences, she who has enjoyed success and universal approbation and has never experienced poverty?' Dr Burney's reaction was even harsher: 'I beg, warn and admonish you not to entangle yourself in a wild and romantic attachment which offers nothing in prospect but poverty and distress.'

Then followed a string of conversions. Narbonne

was won over by Lock, Susan by both of them, and the Queen by her own generosity of spirit. Dr Burney relented only to the extent of giving his cold consent, but refused to attend the wedding.

It took place at 7am on Sunday 28 July 1793 in the little Norman church of Mickleham. Fanny's brother James gave her away in the absence of her father, and William Lock was d'Arblay's best man. Mrs Lock, Narbonne, Susan and her husband were the only other guests. St. Michael's, Mickleham, must be one of the few parish churches in England to commemorate a wedding by a plaque. On it she is described as Fanny, not the formal Frances, and he as 'General' d'Arblay, a rank of which he had been deprived when he fled to England.

The couple rented rooms in a nearby farm before moving four months later to a house in Great Bookham, Surrey. There they remained for four years, so desperately short of money that they lived for a whole week off the vegetables that d'Arblay grew in the garden. He cultivated it without even a wheelbarrow to lighten his labours, and cut the hedges with his sabre. Just before Christmas 1794 a son was born to Fanny. He was christened Alexander, after his father, and was known as Alex.

It was essential that Fanny should begin to earn money by her pen. D'Arblay was of no help except as gardener, baby-sitter and amanuensis for his wife. She had written nothing of commercial value since *Cecilia*, and before embarking on a new novel, she wrote a play called *Edwy and Elgiva*. Although Sarah Siddons, the most famous actress of her day, was the star and it was staged in London's most prestigious theatre, Drury Lane, it was withdrawn after a single performance, Fanny herself acknowledging that the plot lacked incident and the language was stilted.

She then began to write her third novel, *Camilla*. She had sketched the plot while still at Windsor, and wrote it at speed, often late at night, while her husband minded the baby and made fair copies of her manuscripts in his neat hand. It is a long book, 950 pages in a modern edition, and it is reasonable to suppose that she enjoyed the writing of it, as, needing the income so urgently, she could have shortened it. It is a story, once again, of youth and courtship, indiscretion, unhappiness and intrigue. The little moves backwards and forwards between parents and children, lovers and the beloved end happily with Camilla's reconciliation with her lover and her marriage to him. It was a typical 18th-century drama of domestic life, with a huge cast and moral lessons like Fanny's disapproval of society's obsession with good looks. It is a novel of serious intent in which cheerfulness constantly breaks through. In *Northanger Abbey* Jane Austen referred to *Cecilia* and *Camilla* as novels 'in which the most thorough knowledge of human nature, the happiest delineation of its varieties, the liveliest of wit and humour, are conveyed to the world in the best chosen language', but she was half-defending, half-mocking her own trade.

Fanny marketed *Camilla* with great care. The book was still published anonymously 'by the author of *Evelina* and *Cecilia*', but she sold the copyright for £1,000 and earned more than another £1,000 by selling it to subscribers for a guinea each. The first edition, of which I have a copy, contains a list of 1,088 people who had been persuaded to buy the five volumes unseen, including Georgiana Duchess of Devonshire, Edmund

Burke (five sets), Madame de Staël (two sets), Warren Hastings and 'Miss J. Austen, Steventon'. Fanny's success in attracting so distinguished a list is proof not only of her determination but of the survival of her reputation after fourteen silent years. The book sold well, four times as many copies as *Evelina* and nearly double *Cecilia*'s, but it was less successful with the critics who complained of its unnecessary length. One appreciative reader was the Queen, to whom it was dedicated by 'Your Majesty's most obedient, most obliged and most dutiful servant, F. d'Arblay', with apologies that 'the inhabitant of a retired cottage should cast this humble offering at Your Majesty's feet'. Her meeting with the Queen at Windsor to present the volumes was less obsequious. The King joined them, and in his old style began interrogating Fanny. 'What did you write of it here?' he cried. 'How far did you go? Did you finish any part – or only form the skeleton?' 'Just that, sir,' I answered. 'I worked it up in my little cottage. I devoted myself to it wholly – I had no Episode [distraction] but a little baby.' D'Arblay was made to wait outside, but Fanny presented him to the King on the terrace.

With the profits of *Camilla* they built a small house at West Humble, in a field given to them as a wedding present by William Lock, and named it Camilla Cottage. Fanny described it as Lilliputian, but it had three downstairs rooms and four bedrooms. Outside there was an hundred-foot well and a ha-ha dug by d'Arblay in his abundant free time. It cost £1,300 and survived until 1919, when it was accidentally burned to the ground.

It was here that Fanny wrote two more plays, *Love and Fashion*, which though billed for Covent Garden, was never produced, and *A Busy Day*, which remained in manuscript until 1980 and was given its first London performance at the Lyric Theatre in July 2000. The play dealt with some of Fanny's favourite themes, the insolent treatment of women by men, and the vulgarity of the impoverished aristocracy and *nouveaux riches*. It is the liveliest of Fanny's plays, but it reads better than it acts. Regency comedy becomes farce on the modern stage, and the nuances are lost.

In 1800 her favourite correspondent and most loved member of her family, Susan Phillips, died in tragic circumstances. Her husband, Molesworth Phillips, who began his career romantically as a fellow voyager with Captain Cook in the South Seas, had degenerated into an idle, dissolute man. He had resented Susan's involvement with the Juniper group, was unfaithful to her, took to drink and fell deeply into debt. In 1796 he decided to move his family to Ireland where he had inherited a small farm. Susan would have preferred divorce, but for the sake of her children agreed to go with him. Four years later she set off in mid-winter to visit Fanny but had progressed no further than Cheshire, where she died, struck down by dysentery and consumption. The bad roads and weather prevented Fanny from attending her funeral. Instead, she heaped reproaches on Molesworth: 'Oh God, keep me from the sight of that baleful being who can now have the heart – the hard, black heart – to visit all the friends of the Angel he wasted into her tomb.'

V

Fanny's erratic life now took another turn. With her husband and child she went to live in France, and did not return to England for ten years. It was on d'Arblay's insistence that they made this move. He was not unhappy at Camilla Cottage, but even for so unassuming a man it cannot have been an edifying existence to live without money, serious occupation or any position in society, and to be wholly dependent on his wife. He felt himself to be a failure, and a stranger in a foreign land with which his own country was at war. He wished to end his nine-year exile, and his chance came in 1801 when he heard that his property was no longer proscribed by the French Government and he might sell part of his land at Joigny, near Paris, for a maximum of £1,000, provided that he made his claim in writing 'from a country not at war with France'. He chose Holland. Fanny wished to go with him, but the expense, and the danger of a winter journey, deterred her. D'Arblay arrived too late to reclaim his property, and returned to England still penniless, hoping that events might turn in his favour. For once, he was fortunate. In 1802, an armed truce, the Peace of Amiens, was agreed between England and France, and he was free to return to Paris, where he could recover the love of his friends, and possibly his rank and fortune under Napoleon, now First Consul.

Fanny was unwilling to leave her home and family for a country where her situation would be the reverse of her husband's in England, a foreigner without friends or any means of earning an income, and with an English child who would be brought up French. Further, they faced the possibility that the war would be resumed, and she would be in permanent exile. All these obstacles she confronted calmly, and decided that her duty and love for d'Arblay must predominate.

D'Arblay, who went ahead, was welcomed in Paris by Lafayette, Narbonne and de Staël, all by now fervent Bonapartists, and they canvassed for his reinstatement. Napoleon replied, through Berthier, his Minister of

War, that he must earn his rehabilitation by military service. He must join an overseas expedition, perhaps to San Domingo, and a wound would help ('*qu'il revient avec une blessure*'). Then he would be regarded with favour by the Army and could be restored on half pay to his rank as Chef de Brigade. D'Arblay replied that he had sworn never to bear arms against England – '*la patrie de mon épouse, le pays que pendant 9 ans nous a nourris*'. Napoleon answered that this is what he would have expected from '*le mari de Cecilia*', but he could not grant restitution under that condition. Fanny, before she left England to rejoin him, begged him to avoid fighting of any kind:

I dread any effort of courage, a *désir d'une blessure*, more than words can say – ah remember, *une blessure* is most commonly but a lingering death... I wish to give you a thousand blessings – and not one pain – but the flutter of my spirits is inconceivable. Tenderest tears of a creature wholly your's. F. d'A.

D'Arblay, who lacked the martial spirit, agreed. He

bought a new uniform to which he was not yet entitled and could ill afford.

While the peace still held, Fanny renovated Camilla Cottage and let it to strangers, and in April 1802 set out with little Alex to join her husband. It was her first journey abroad. Exile was not banishment. She wrote to him from Calais in the bilingual patois they had adopted, '*J'arrive, mon ami, mon Cher – Cher ami*! – frightened – harassed – embarrassed, but eager, happy, and with a whole soul beating with truest tenderness – *j'arrive pour ne jamais vous quitter*.' Her first impression of France was favourable – 'Their decency, their silence, their quietness astonished me' – for she had been expecting hostile revolutionaries, and when a band struck up 'God Save the King' outside her hotel, she could scarcely believe that she was in France.

Within a fortnight of her arrival in Paris, she came face to face with Napoleon. She described the encounter in one of the most famous of the set pieces in her journal-letters, this one addressed to her father. Accustomed as she was to royal trappings, she was amazed by the splendour of the Tuileries and, confronted by her country's enemy, she could not help but be deeply impressed by him. Her party had tickets for one of the great apartments in the palace, and she waited there for the First Consul to pass through on his way to take the salute on the parade ground below its windows. The room was so crowded that she feared that she would miss 'even a passing peep' at him, but d'Arblay's influence gained her admission to a smaller room reserved for more privileged guests. There she stood among the generals when Napoleon entered by the far door:

Not a soul either spoke or stirred as he and his suite passed along: which was so quickly that had I not been placed so near the door, I could hardly have seen him. As it was, I had a view so near, though so brief, of his face, as to be very much struck by it. It is of a deeply impressive cast, pale even to sallowness, while not only in the eye, but in every feature, Care, Thought, Melancholy and Meditation are strongly marked, with so much of character, nay Genius, and so penetrating a seriousness – or rather sadness, as powerfully to sink into an observer's mind – yet, though the busts and medallions I have seen are, in general, such good resemblances, I think I should have known him untold.

Most people, on seeing Napoleon for the first time, were so influenced by their knowledge of his extraordinary career that they had already formed a notion of his character – he must be an exceptionally powerful man. Fanny's impression was different:

> The look of the commander who heads his own army, who fights his own battles, who conquers every difficulty by personal exertion, who executes all his plans, who performs even all he suggests – whose ambition is of the most enterprising and whose bravery is of the most daring cast – this the spectator watches for in vain. He has far more the air of a student than of a warrior.

She was to change her opinion when she became aware of Napoleon's tyranny and, after the failure of his Russian campaign, of his vulnerability, but her admiration of him never quite faded. When shown Jacques-Louis David's equestrian portrait of him, she dwelled on his imperturbable composure. 'He seems absorbed in ruminations so abstruse that they lift him above all personal care and give him a contempt of all personal danger.' This from a woman who was otherwise indifferent to masculine display, and regarded war only as something that her husband should avoid.

When hostilities broke out again in May 1803 she was never molested for her nationality and came to honour the French for their kindness to her. But she was distraught at finding herself virtually an enemy in an alien country. Napoleon decreed that all English people between the ages of 18 and 60 were to be regarded as prisoners of war; they were forbidden to write letters to England, or receive any from their families. Thus she was kept in total ignorance of the progress of the war. She did not hear of Nelson's victory at Trafalgar until seven years after the battle. She received no money. Her royal pension was suspended and the rent for Camilla Cottage left unpaid. D'Arblay was obliged to take the humblest of clerical jobs at the Ministry of the Interior which paid him little more in francs than the equivalent of £100 a year. Her novels were well known in Paris, but her reticence prevented her from benefiting from her fame. D'Arblay was not insensitive to Fanny's distress. He hoped to distract her by the society of his aristocratic friends and afford her the pleasures of the city as far as his exiguous income would allow. But she did not need entertainment, and never spoke French fluently enough to make her easy in company. 'My voice', she wrote, 'is as wearied of pronouncing as my brain is wearied of searching for words to pronounce.' Her main occupation was caring for her son Alex. He was unsociable, often ill, but was remarkably hard-working and bright. At his Paris school he won so many credit marks that he was allowed to pass on some of them to his fellow-pupils to offset against their bad marks, so that they would be released to go home for the holidays. When he won six major awards at the annual prize-giving even the students joined in the applause, and Fanny, who was unable to conceal her adoration of him, did nothing to curb his conceit. Alex's success went to his head. He became the masters' favourite pupil, a sure way to unpopularity in the school.

Their subdued existence in Paris was interrupted by

an event for which, if she had written nothing else, Fanny Burney would be remembered. She underwent, without anaesthetic, the removal of her right breast. Mastectomy was not an unprecedented operation; what was unprecedented was her description of it. She wrote it nine months after her recovery in the form of a letter to Esther (Hetty), recalling everything that was said and left unsaid, and sparing her sister no detail of her ordeal. It was omitted from the first edition of her journals (1846) as it was thought to be too shocking.

As always in Fanny's set pieces, she delayed the culmination by a lengthy narrative of the preliminaries in order to build up for the reader the tension of the sufferer. For some time, in the summer of 1810, she had been experiencing slight pains in her breast, and felt within it a swelling lump. She was persuaded by d'Arblay to consult a doctor, Antoine Dubois, one of the most celebrated surgeons in France and gynaecologist to the Empress Josephine. She wrote, 'I had much difficulty in telling myself what he endeavoured not to tell me – that a small operation would be necessary.' A second opinion was sought. Narbonne persuaded

Dominique Larrey, chief surgeon to the Imperial Guard, to examine her, and he in turn brought in Dr François Ribes, the anatomist, and another doctor, Jacques-Louis Moreau. The attention given to her, a foreigner declared an enemy, by these distinguished men bears witness to the extraordinary affection which the d'Arblays had created for themselves in France.

In conference they corroborated Dubois' opinion: an operation was essential. The greater pain of the surgery would remove the lesser pain of the cancer, and it would save her life. Dubois did not conceal from her what she must endure. '*Il faut s'attendre à souffrir. Je ne veux pas vous tromper. Vous souffrirez – vous souffrirez beaucoup.*' Dr Moreau asked her if she cried with pain when Alex was born. Yes, she had; it had not been possible to do otherwise. Good, they said. She must not restrain her screams. She made it a condition that her husband should not witness the operation. They agreed. She asked that she should not be warned of it until two hours before it was due to take place. They agreed to this too, and preparations were made to convert the *salon* of their apartment into a temporary operating theatre. Fanny made her Will.

When the day came, 30 September 1811, d'Arblay was called away from the house on some pretext and Fanny was conducted into the room, followed by seven men in black, the surgeons and two pupils, and one or two nurses. Why so many? There was no time for lengthy explanations. Then she saw that two old mattresses covered by a sheet had been prepared for her to lie on. She was given a wine cordial, the effect of which as an analgesic was negligible. She was told to undress, and lie down. They offered to bind her to prevent her struggling. She refused. They put a cambric handkerchief over her eyes. It was semi-transparent, and through it she watched the doctors gather round. She saw the glitter of polished steel. She closed her eyes. There was a pause, and then Dr Larrey said; '*Qui me tiendra ce sein?*' ['Who will support the breast?'] Fanny sprang up, crying, '*C'est moi, monsieur!*', held her hand under it, and the operation began.

'My dear Esther,' she wrote, 'when the dreadful steel was plunged into the breast – cutting through veins, arteries, flesh, nerves – I needed no injunctions not to restrain my cries. I began a scream that lasted unintermittingly during the whole time of the incision – and I almost marvel that it rings not in my ears still, so excruciating was the agony. When the wound was made and the instrument was withdrawn, the pain seemed undiminished – but when again I felt the knife, describing a curve, cutting against the grain, if I may say so, then indeed I thought I must have expired. The instrument this second time withdrawn, I concluded the operation over. Oh no! Presently the terrible cutting was renewed – and worse than ever, to separate the bottom, the foundation of this dreadful gland, from the parts to which it adhered. I felt the knife rackling against the breast-bone – scraping it! – I remained in utterly speechless torture.'

Her whole breast was removed, not just the tumour as she had expected. The operation lasted 20 minutes. Twice she momentarily fainted, but in spite of her unspeakable suffering, not once did she resist. Every instinct must have induced her to brush away the surgeon's hand; just as we, who benefit from every modern form of pain relief, resist the dentist's drill. While undergoing this torture, she cried aloud, '*Ah Messieurs!*

Que je vous plains!' ['How I pity you!'], knowing what they must be suffering from being obliged to inflict such suffering on her. The official report ended, '*L'opération a été très douloureuse, et supportée avec un grand courage.*' Fanny was 59 years old, and lived another 29 without any recurrence of the cancer.

Her recovery was quick, and she soon resumed work on the novel which she had started as long ago as 1799 – before she went to France. It was called *The Wanderer*. One might have expected it to be about her experiences in France, but it was about England. Not the England to which she longed to return, but an unpleasant country where injustice, if not tyranny, permeated society. She returned with renewed vigour to her attack on the ill-treatment of women by men, of the poor by the rich. The heroine Ellis, who would not give her true name, escapes from France to England, finds it dull, stuffy, snobbish and cruel. She teaches the harp. Her pupils will not pay her fees, arguing that it was a privilege for her to teach them, a luxury for both, that deserved no payment. So she takes to millinery, and is thereby further degraded. To sew was ladylike: to sew for money was disgraceful. But Ellis is a finer person than her persecutors, the daughter, as it turns out, of an English peer, cleverer than them, more vibrant, more adventurous. She allows to the peasantry, even poorer than herself, the dignity that evades the rich.

In one sense it is a political novel. When it was published in 1814, the critics abused it for the very quality that makes it great, its passionate condemnation of injustice. The *Quarterly Review* said that it lacked 'all vigour, vivacity and originality'. William Hazlitt called her characters 'whether of refinement or vulgarity, equally superficial and confined', and Byron dismissed it as 'feminine trash'. Macaulay much later said that 'no friend of Miss Burney could rescue it from the oblivion into which it has justly fallen.' The public reflected this general air of censure. There was disappointment that she had not repeated the manner of her earlier and sprightlier books. *The Wanderer* deserved better than that. Kate Chisholm, one of Fanny's most recent biographers, is justified in concluding, 'This is her richest and most rewarding book.' But it did not sell well. The first edition, on the strength of Fanny's name, was soon exhausted, but the second was pulped when half remained unsold, and the book was not reprinted until 1988. She made from it £1,500, but it had taken her fifteen years to write.

In August 1812 Fanny had returned to England carrying with her the half-completed manuscript of her novel. Her passport was drawn up in such a way that she was obliged to travel from Dunkirk in a ship bound for New York, which might, illegally, drop her off at Dover. By an odd twist of fortune, even this plan was thwarted by the Royal Navy which intercepted the ship in mid-Channel, because England was now at war with the United States, and forced the passengers to land at Deal. This suited Fanny admirably. But just as she had been suspected in France of being an English spy, now she was suspected of being a French spy in England. Fortunately there were local people who had known her at Norbury Park, and she was sent on her way to London. Her brother, Charles, who had been waiting for her at Dover, caught up with her *en route*, failing at first to recognise her. A stout woman of 60 was not the Cecilia he remembered.

She found her father in a state of decline. He had suffered a stroke. His head hung down, and he was very deaf. After catching up with the family news and meeting old friends like George Cambridge, Fanny turned with her usual promptitude to business. She hurriedly completed her novel, arranged for its publication, managed to secure for Alex a place at Caius College, Cambridge, and went down to Surrey to inspect Camilla Cottage, which she found in perfect condition. She intended to make it her future home, but discovered, to her intense annoyance, that the deeds had not been properly drawn up at the time of her marriage, and the land on which the cottage stood was still the property of the Locks. William Lock had died, and his son was selling the Norbury estate, Camilla Cottage with it. She had no home.

Dr Burney died at Chelsea College in April 1814, so peacefully that Fanny, who was sitting at his bedside, did not realise for two hours that he was dead, rather than sleeping. He had been able to hold in his hands a copy of *The Wanderer* and note the dedication to himself, by name, in contrast to the anonymity of her dedication to him in *Evelina,* but still her own name did not appear on the title-page.

In her absence, great events had occurred in France. The Allies marched on Paris, and the French army, weakened by desertions and constant battles, allowed them to enter the city unopposed; while Napoleon retreated to Fontainebleau, where he abdicated in April. Louis XVIII was declared King again, with Talleyrand as his Prime Minister. D'Arblay was free to come to London to comfort Fanny in her bereavement. Their financial situation was now slightly better. There were the royalties from *The Wanderer* and Dr Burney had left Fanny £1,000 in his Will. Their share of the sale of Camilla Cottage had come to £650. For the moment they remained in London, in the hope that d'Arblay might be appointed French Consul there, an ambition in which he was disappointed. But he was given a commission in the Guards and, at last restored to his profession, he returned to Paris.

Fanny met the French King as he was on his way from his English retreat to claim his throne. The audience took place in Grillion's Hotel, off Piccadilly. Though too timid to push herself forward, she was eager to see what was going on. The King advanced 'slowly, slowly, slowly, rather dragging his legs and weak limbs than walking', and a courtier, the Duc de Duras, spotting Fanny in the crowd, insisted on presenting her: 'Sire, Madame d'Arblay.' She wrote:

When His Majesty raised his eyes with a look of pleased curiosity at my name, and took my hand, and said in very pretty English, 'I am very happy to see you,' I felt such a glow of satisfaction that, involuntarily, I burst forth with its expression. He added that he had known me very long, 'for I have *read* you – and been charmed with your books. I know them very well, indeed, and have long wanted to know you.'

In saying goodbye to her, the King addressed her as Madame La Comtesse, thus indicating the restoration of her husband's title. It was subtly done. In truth, d'Arblay did not benefit greatly from the change. His rank in the Royal Guard was no higher than that of sub-lieutenant, carrying with it derisory pay, and the Guard was considered by the rest of the Army a slightly absurd body of has-beens, unfit for serious campaigning. But d'Arblay was ecstatic. He brought Fanny to Paris once again, in the expectation of peace, comfort and promotion.

Then, on 1 March 1815, Napoleon escaped from Elba.

V1

At first Paris remained calm. Louis XVIII swore publicly never to yield his throne, and sent Marshal Ney south to bring Napoleon back 'in an iron cage'. D'Arblay, magnificent in his new uniform, drove Fanny every day through the Bois de Boulogne. There was no panic. The royalists laughed at Napoleon's 'escapade'. Then came the news that Ney had changed sides, and that Napoleon had been received with raptures at Lyon. The royalist army began to desert. A civil war was thought inevitable. There was talk of a great battle south of Paris, but none took place. Napoleon entered the capital unopposed on 20 March and, as Emperor once again, reoccupied the Tuileries. The King fled to Belgium, and his Garde de Corps went with him.

Alexandre d'Arblay did not strike a heroic figure at this crisis. His position was anomalous. Once a declared supporter of Napoleon, he was now a royalist general with a lieutenant's pay. He was prepared to fight, but his King fled the field. His men cried 'Vive...', but then paused, uncertain how to complete the sentence. D'Arblay begged Fanny to make her way to England because in France she was doubly in danger, as an Englishwoman and the wife of a royalist soldier. They had a most affecting farewell. They knelt together, praying for each other's safety. In later years Fanny re-collected:

How dreadful was our parting. At the door he turned back and with a smile, which though forced, had the inexpressible sweetness of approvance, he half gaily exclaimed, 'Vive le Roi!', and then he darted from my sight... I ran to the window which looked upon the inward courtyard. There, indeed, behold him I did – but Oh with what anguish! Just mounting his war-horse – a noble animal but which at this moment I viewed with acutest terror, for it seemed loaded with pistols, and equipped completely for immediate service on the field of battle.

Of course there was no battle. D'Arblay had no

choice but to follow his Sovereign ignominiously into exile. He made for Ghent, Fanny for Brussels, leaving all her precious papers and possessions in Paris. Such was the ambiguity of her situation that her passport was made out in the name of Madame d'Arblay, *née* Burney, with no mention of her husband. She travelled with a friend, Princesse d'Hénin, in a coach drawn by four horses and escorted by four servants, through Amiens to Arras. It was a nightmare journey in the dark, on rutted roads. The Princess was silent, nervous and, when she spoke, invariably grumpy, more concerned with the safety of her luggage than the fate of kings. Officials on the road were unwilling to give them much help, being uncertain whether they still had the authority, and waiting, as Fanny put it, until *le droit du plus fort* decided who were their masters.

Eventually they crossed the frontier into Belgium, and at Tournai found rest and relief in a commodious inn. Fanny set out to discover what had happened to the Garde Royale. Were they with the King? Where was he? But everyone to whom she applied for help was too wrapped up in their own anxieties to care much about a stranger's. The only person who treated her with sympathy was the Viscomte Chateaubriand, who by chance was lodging in the same inn. He was one of Louis XVIII's new ministers, and later French Ambassador in London, but Fanny knew him as the most outstanding literary genius of his time. She had never met him before, and perhaps expressed her gratitude for his books and help too fulsomely, for he hung back, 'whether pleased or not, with an air of gentlemanly serenity'. She gives us no hint that he had ever heard of her.

On reaching Brussels, they rented a house near the cathedral, and Fanny renewed her efforts to discover her husband's whereabouts. He was at Ypres, just inside the Belgian frontier, having arrived there without his warhorse and weakened by his ordeals. They finally found each other through letters addressed to friends who might know where the other was, and then exchanged long accounts of their adventures. D'Arblay explained that he was still attached to the King's Guard, and had command of a battery of artillery that was destined never to fire a shot. Then he was commissioned to go to Trèves (Trier) on the Prussian border, with vague instructions to recruit deserters from Napoleon's army, if there were any. Before leaving for this inglorious assignment he was allowed three weeks leave to join Fanny in Brussels.

Their reunion was touchingly joyful. They were able – but given their penury and loss of possessions it is puzzling to see how – to lead a social life in Brussels little different from that in Paris. They drove in the park, attended church and, as one last treat before they parted, were invited to a concert patronised by the elite of Belgian society and the occupying armies, including the Queen of the Netherlands and the Duke of Wellington himself.

Fanny was always captivated by a famous name, and recorded her impressions of the Duke as much for her own delight in composition as for posterity. She 'looked at him watchfully all night, and was charmed with every turn of his countenance, with his noble and singular physiognomy', noting the famous eagle eye and aquiline nose, and observed his easy relationship with his officers, talking to all of them with 'a sort of reserved intimacy', and how charmed he was by the star of the concert, Angelica Catalani, until she sang 'Rule Britannia', of which he forbade an encore, with obvious consideration for the Queen, whose guest he nominally was. Fanny, to whom he did not address a word, was deeply impressed by this gesture, which 'offered me an opportunity to seeing how magnificently he could quit his convivial familiarity for imperious dominion'. She was seeing him, presciently, as the character he was to become in *Vanity Fair*. Thackeray, indeed, used Fanny's journals of this period as a palette for his novel.

D'Arblay left her for Trèves, she feeling the relief, he the shame, that he would be absent from the inevitable battle outside Brussels. She remained in the city awaiting it. Once, when walking in the park, she saw the famous Caroline Lamb, and was shocked by her appearance, designed to attract officers and men, 'one shoulder, half her back, and all her throat and neck displayed as if at the call of some statuary for modelling a heathen goddess'. But no distractions of this kind could lift the suspense. It was known that Napoleon had crossed the frontier into Belgium, with Brussels as his objective.

Spies, deserters and rumours proliferated in the city, and then, on 16 June 1815, the blow fell.

Fanny's account of the Waterloo campaign was written eight years later, from memory and from her letters to d'Arblay. Nobody who had experienced such anxieties in such dramatic circumstances needed to embellish her story in recollection, least of all one possessed of such acute powers of recall as Fanny Burney. She was able to record not just the highlights, but every moment of confusion and despond. The authenticity of her account is confirmed by details that no myth-maker would invent. The battles were taking place not ten miles from where she lived. She could hear the cannonade and every conflicting account of it, at one moment awaiting capture by a victorious Napoleon, at the next expecting Wellington in triumph. The citizens of Brussels seemed silently to favour Napoleon's chances, thinking him invincible. Her consolation was that the postal services between Trèves and Brussels were surprisingly uninterrupted, but she cautioned d'Arblay to address his letters to her as 'Madame de Burney', just in case Brussels fell to the enemy. Risky though the alternatives were, it was safer to be an Englishwoman.

During these four extraordinary days, 16-19 June 1815, Fanny lived in the centre of the city, watching from her window or the doorway of a shop in the Grande Place the solemn procession of soldiers on their way to battle. The news which today would be suppressed for security reasons was delayed by the poverty of communications. The outcome of the battle was so much in the balance that every rumour was instantly believed. A bunch of French prisoners was mistaken for the advance guard of a victorious army. Deserters and runaways excused their cowardice by shouting to bystanders that all was lost. Fanny was among the most ignorant of them. D'Arblay, from his distant frontier-post, could tell her nothing that she was not witnessing with her own eyes and, given her unimportance in this crisis, she had no privileged access to information. She was not among the guests invited by the Duchess of Richmond to the most famous pre-battle ball in history. She heard only long afterwards of the fighting at Quatre Bras on 16 June, when the Duke of Brunswick was killed and Wellington was nearly captured. She had no idea that on the next day the Duke was writing to Sir Charles Stuart, the British Ambassador in Brussels, that the Allies might be obliged to retreat and 'uncover' the city, which meant surrender it. She was unaware that Baron Larrey, who had removed her breast, was three times wounded, taken prisoner and only saved from instant execution by the intervention of a Prussian officer who recognised him. Nor did she hear Louis XVIII's cry from Ghent, in what must count as history's least inspiring call-to-arms, 'Let those who are afraid depart. For myself, I shall not leave here unless forced to do so by the march of events.'

Fanny and her English friends, Walter and Harriet Boyd, decided to make for Antwerp, where they would be within reach of Brussels should the Allies be victorious or of England should they lose. They were to go by barge along the canals. Early in the morning of 18 June, Waterloo day, they set out for the wharf, only to find that all the barges had been commandeered by the military to transport their stores and wounded to Antwerp in anticipation of defeat. On their way back to the city centre they listened to the guns:

The dread reverberations became louder and louder as we proceeded. Every shot tolled to our imaginations the death of myriads, and the probability that if all attempts at escape should prove abortive, we might be personally involved in the carnage, gave us all sensations too awful for verbal expression.

Yet the city remained quiet. When they sought other methods of flight, they were told that all wheeled transport was requisitioned by the Army, and horses were selling for a prince's ransom. They were trapped. It was Sunday, but there could be no thought of church. Then suddenly, at about three in the afternoon, when the battle was at its height at Waterloo, the streets filled with people shouting that the French were come! Fanny, never at a loss for a phrase at a moment of crisis, declared that 'nations waited to know their masters from the trumpet of the victor.' When night fell, the good news was at last confirmed. Wellington and Blücher had met in victory on the field of battle, and Napoleon was in flight. Then began the procession of the wounded and the more distinguished dead:

I never approached my window but to witness sights of wretchedness. Maimed, wounded, bleeding, mutilated, tortured victims of this exterminating contest passed by every minute – the fainting, the sick, the dying and the dead, on brancards, in carts, in wagons...They bit their own cloths, perhaps their flesh, to save the loud emission of their groans.

The whole city turned into a hospital, and Fanny, like every other woman, gave what help she could, winding lint and bandages, and stifling the stench of gangrene by holding to her nose handkerchiefs drenched in eau de Cologne.

She remained a month in Brussels, hearing almost daily from d'Arblay, and on receiving the news that he had been badly injured in the leg by a kick from his horse, made worse by an incompetent surgeon, she determined to join him at Trèves. The journey, for a woman of 63, was very arduous. First there was the renewed difficulty of passports. She would be obliged to travel through Belgium, Prussia and France, when all three were in turmoil. Which would be safer, English by birth or French by marriage? She decided on the latter, but found that the Prussian officials would not accept her passport, until she dropped the name of Kleist, a Prussian general with whom she had a vague acquaintance. Then there was the rarity and unpredictability of public transport. Chance took her by a roundabout route through Liège, Cologne and the Prussian Rhineland. She was subjected to constant delays and bureaucratic indifference, sometimes verging on hostility, but her energy and determination saw her through. Her worst experience was in Bonn. While the coach was delayed for a couple of hours, she went sightseeing, got lost, could not ask her way for lack of adequate German, and was desperately worried that the coach would leave without her, and she would be stranded without luggage, money, friends or knowledge of the language. By good fortune she stumbled on the hotel where she had dismounted, just as the diligence (stagecoach) was leaving. She enjoyed the trip down the Rhine with 'its mountains, towers, castles, fortifications, country-houses and picturesque villages'. She was besotted by the romance of it. But at Coblenz there was more trouble. A new visa was required, and this could not be obtained until it was too late for her to catch the diligence for Trèves that was leaving early next morning. It would be a week before another left. She was in despair. She insisted on seeing the authorities who issued visas. Impossible. They were old men who would be in bed. Nevertheless, with a willing boy as guide, she found her way to the house of the Prussian commandant, pleaded with his officers that her cause was desperate and obtained his signature. Now she had to gather the counter-signature of the chief of the German police. She was led to his house. He was in bed, fast asleep, and could not be disturbed. She forced her way into his bedroom, again pronounced the name of General Kleist, her husband's 'intimate friend', and this was enough to gain his grudging assent. With her last half-napoleon she bought a passage for the remaining 100 kilometres to Trèves, where she arrived on 24 July, wondering whether d'Arblay was still alive. He was, though very weak. Their meeting, she wrote, was one of 'exquisite felicity'.

They spent a month together at Trèves, where d'Arblay was still ostensibly on active service for the

King, who now made him not only a count, as he had half-promised Fanny, but a lieutenant general. He slowly convalesced while Fanny enjoyed the beauty of the Moselle valley. Then they went to Paris to celebrate the second restoration of the King. The journey through France, by permission of its liberators, was accomplished with difficulty, for in spite of his credentials and evident pain, d'Arblay was treated with offensive disdain by the Prussian and Russian officials along the route. Fanny happened to pass the farmhouse where the Czar Alexander I was temporarily lodging and, with her serendipitous good fortune, she saw him emerge as she stood staring at the gate. There had to be a pen-portrait.

The Emperor came out, in an undress uniform, wearing no stars or orders, or none visible, and with an air of gay good humour and unassuming ease and liveliness. He seemed in blyth and flowering health, and replete with happiness. There was something in his whole appearance of hilarity, freedom, youthfulness and total absence of all thought of state or power.

They arrived in Paris to find it in the hands of the British. Their apartment was untouched, and Baron Larrey, recovered from his own wounds, came to tend d'Arblay's leg. They renewed their friendships with the Princesse d'Hénin, Lafayette and many others and, after a gap of 22 years, met Talleyrand, now Foreign Minister to the King. He did not recognise her, but as she passed his chair, she murmured, '*M. de Talleyrand m'a oublié, mais on n'oublié pas M. de Talleyrand.*' He looked up, puzzled, but they did not speak.

VII

They returned to London in October 1815, intending to make England their home for the rest of their lives, since it was more settled than France and Alex was there. They decided to make Bath their base, chiefly because Fanny retained such happy memories of her three-month visit there with Mrs Thrale, and d'Arblay's leg wound, which refused to heal, might benefit from the waters. It was the ideal town for retired people of slender means. No carriage would be necessary, as shops and friends were all to be found within walking distance. The streets were clean, the people honest and a beautiful countryside was within easy reach. They took lodgings at 23 Great Stanhope Street on the way to Bristol. There they had two floors of a small house, and managed to exist on an exiguous income, perhaps £300 from their investments and the £100 which the Court still paid Fanny as a pension. D'Arblay contributed very little. On returning to Paris in 1817 to collect his arrears of pay he came back with almost nothing except a portrait of himself by Carl Vernet, now at Parham House in Sussex. It symbolises the lopsided nature of their marriage, for he told Fanny, pathetically, that he had had it painted primarily for their son who might otherwise forget that he had a father as well as a mother. It depicts him in the full uniform of a general. A war-horse waits behind him, and a battle scene (Waterloo?) is sketched in the background to suggest the glory that he might have won if given the chance. The epaulettes, collar and cuffs which he was wearing for the portrait are preserved in a glass case beneath it.

They lived very quietly in Bath, hampered by their poverty and d'Arblay's lameness. An expedition to the Pump Room was exceptional, and they seldom climbed to the Circus or Royal Crescent, being unable to afford a sedan-chair, the most inefficient vehicle ever devised, for it required two men to carry one. D'Arblay was able to do a little work in an allotment, and Fanny began to sort out her father's papers. She wrote little but read widely. It is one of the mysteries of literary history that never once in her diaries and letters did she mention any of Jane Austen's novels, although two of them, *Northanger Abbey* and *Persuasion*, were set partly in Bath, and Fanny was a close friend of Cassandra Cooke, a first cousin of Jane Austen's mother, who must inevitably have spoken about them since all six of the novels were published just before, or during, Fanny's residence there.

There were two encounters that recalled her past. The first was with Mrs Piozzi, the former Mrs Thrale, with whom Fanny had quarrelled so deeply 31 years before. Widowed for the second time, Mrs Piozzi took rooms in Gay Street, a fashionable part of Bath, and Fanny called on her. She was received coldly at first, but Mrs Piozzi melted when they began to reminisce, 'with all her old facility and pleasantry and singularity', [Fanny wrote to Lady Keith, Mrs Piozzi's daughter], 'and we talked, both of us, in Dr Johnson's phrase "our best", but entirely as two strangers, who had no sort of knowledge or care for each other, but were willing each to fling and to accept the gauntlet.' As Fanny was leaving, Mrs Piozzi's manner changed. She cried out, 'Thank you and God bless you,' and Fanny turned back to press her hand. On Mrs Piozzi's side, however, there was less forgiveness. She wrote in her diary, 'She is very charming, she always was, but I will never trust her more.'

The second encounter was with Queen Charlotte. In November 1817 she came to Bath without the King, who was by now mentally incapacitated, and wherever she went during her four-day visit she was received with acclamation, muted only by the news that Princess Charlotte, the Queen's granddaughter, had died in childbirth. The elaborate Guildhall banquet was cancelled. After the funeral the Queen returned to Bath and stayed a month. She sent a message to Fanny that she wished to meet General d'Arblay, and he forgot his pains sufficiently to converse with her in the Pump Room, then sank back to a bench. 'He could stand no longer,' reported Fanny, 'and we returned home to spend the rest of the day in bodily misery.' It was not the last of her meetings with the Queen. She called on her daily in the modest lodgings which she had taken in Sydney Place, where the Austens had lived for four years, and found no difficulty in recapturing the deferential manner of the Court. Her references to the Queen, now as always, exceeded in adulation what the circumstances required: 'Her grace was indescribable, and to those who never witnessed it, inconceivable, for it was such as to carry off age, infirmity, sickness, ugliness, diminutive and disproportionate stature [the Mayor of Bath was 75 years old and only four foot tall], and to give to her a power of charming and delighting that rarely has been equalled.' It was Fanny's farewell to her. Queen Charlotte died at Windsor in November 1818.

General d'Arblay did not long survive this royal accolade. His health steadily deteriorated through the winter of 1817-18, and he died on 3 May, aged 65. We know a great deal about his decline because Fanny, in one of the most remarkable of her retrospective journals, recorded it in 25,000 words. It is an extraordinary document, comparable to her 'Mastectomy', being both a narrative of events 'for the family archive' and a eulogy of her husband. John Wiltshire, who has analysed it carefully [*Literature and Medicine* 12 No. 2 (1993)], calls it 'a harrowing experience enwrapped in

the packaging of romance'. Fanny herself is its unde-
clared heroine, acting until the last days as her husband's sole nurse, indefatigably courageous, refusing
to give up hope even when the doctors despaired.
She wrote little about d'Arblay's illness and treatment,
because she could not bring herself to admit that he was
suffering from an inoperable cancer of the rectum. She
invented tests to reassure both of them, like holding out
a lighted match for him to blow out, to show that his
lungs were unaffected. D'Arblay knew well enough that
he was dying. He put his papers in order, and tried to
prepare Fanny for the inevitable. At one moment only
did he seem to challenge her self-delusion, calling out,
'Oh Fanny, Fanny, what is become of your veracity?'

Towards the end, a priest was called to hear his con-
fession, and remained with the dying man for three
hours. Fanny resented his intrusion, though d'Arblay
had requested it, because he was a Catholic and his
presence suggested a calamity which she still could not
bring herself to accept. The priest returned to give him
the last sacrament and then, in Fanny's words, her
husband,

bent forward, and taking my hand and holding it between his own hands, with a smile celestial, a look composed, serene, benign – even radiant, he impressively said, '*Je ne sais si ce sera le dernier mot – mais ce sera la dernière pensée – Notre Réunion!*'

She was at his bedside, but just as when her father died, for two hours she did not recognise it for what it was. She felt his feet grow cold and sought to warm them with flannel cloths, and it was only when the doctor came to feel his pulse, and found none, that she gave way to her despair.

She buried him at Bath, in the cemetery of St. Swithin's, Walcot, a Protestant church as he had requested, so that Fanny and Alex could in time join him there. She commissioned a headstone, and within the church placed a large marble tablet which recorded his honours and personality in affectionate hyperbole. The first few lines were in French ('... *Lieutenant General des Armées et Officier Supérieur des Gardes de Corps de S. M. Louis XVIII, Roi de France*'), the rest in English, celebrating 'the indescribable charm of his social virtues' and other attributes. Fanny had never reproached him for being so ineffectual a husband, because he was cultured, high-minded and loved her, and she loved him. He did not make a Will because he had nothing to bequeath to her except his portrait as the warrior he never became.

Their son Alex was also at his father's deathbed, and was regarded by Fanny as her main source of consolation. He was an unusual young man. He had done well at Cambridge, earning a Fellowship at Christ's College as a competent mathematician and linguist, capable of debating mathematical theory for three hours in Latin, but he had no ambition. He was an attractive idler, a poet, a wanderer, with 'a sweet and guileless temper' as a contemporary described him. Fanny wished sometimes that he had been born a girl, to keep her company in old age, and though his disposition was indeed more feminine than masculine (Margaret Doody has suggested that 'he may have been homosexual without quite knowing it'), he resented her attempts to manage every detail of his life. She was, after all, old enough to be his grandmother. So he spent much time abroad, roaming the Continent a little fecklessly and writing his mother very few letters. When it became essential for him to adopt some profession, he was ordained in 1819 without much enthusiasm and took a series of curacies, first at Camden Chapel at a salary of £150, then at Hartwell, Buckinghamshire, to stand in for an absent vicar, and finally in Holborn, a parish which George Cambridge obtained for him, possibly in compensation for disappointing Fanny fifty years before. Alex did not take his duties very seriously, preferring chess, Byron's poetry and the company of women to preaching sermons and there were complaints that he did not turn up for his own services. Several times he fell in love, but was too poor to marry. Towards the end, he became engaged half-heartedly to Mary Ann Smith, but before they could marry he caught a cold and died, aged 42. It was an unfulfilled life, redeemed by his endearing personality. He had been fond of his mother, but she had loved him to excess, and wished on him ambitions that he did not share,

Soon after she was widowed, Fanny decided to leave

Bath for London. Bath now held few attractions for her, and she thought it an unsuitable place for Alex whom she imagined blossoming in the metropolis. Her only regret on leaving Bath was that her sister Esther (Hetty) also lived there, but in London she would have the company of her brother James, now an admiral, and a few others with whom she had maintained friendships, notably the Princesses, daughters of George III, who showed her exemplary kindness, sending warmed carriages to bring her to the London palaces and Windsor for a day's reminiscence. After a long period in mourning, she began once again to frequent society, and in a modest way to entertain. She lived in the most fashionable part of Mayfair, first at 11 Bolton Street, Piccadilly, where a modern plaque records her residence, then successively at 1 Half Moon Street, 112 Mount Street and 29 Lower Grosvenor Street, where she died. Hers was still a name to arouse interest and respect, more for her first two novels and friendship with the Johnson circle than for her later adventures, since the existence of her journals was unknown. Walter Scott, an admirer, came to see her, and was impressed by her 'simple and apparently amiable manners with quick feelings', and wrote in his diary, 'She is an elderly lady with no remains of personal beauty, but with a gentle manner and a pleasing expression of countenance.' She told him how she had danced round the mulberry tree in her father's garden when she heard of the success of *Evelina*, a story which some of her biographers think invented, but if it was a myth, it was excusable. In old age Fanny became an indefatigable talker and reminiscence improves with the telling.

She did not neglect her writing. It still amused her to record in letters to her sisters incidents like a holiday in Ilfracombe and a visit to a law-office in the City, having lost little of her gift for ridicule. Her major literary occupation was the compilation of the *Memoirs of Dr Burney*. Her father had left twelve autobiographical notebooks, which she supplemented by her own letters and memories, the letters of her sister Susan and other papers, and she worked on them for twelve years before publishing the *Memoirs* in three volumes in 1832. Her purpose was filial, to burnish his reputation as a serious musical scholar and companion of his distinguished contemporaries, and she did not hesitate to exclude, and burn, passages in the notebooks which did not match this image or, as she described them, the 'peccant parts'. She was determined to present him as a great man, and 'all thought utterly irrelevant, or in any way mischievous, I have committed to the flames', a practice for which she has since been almost universally condemned. Claire Harman, a most sympathetic biographer of Fanny, calls the *Memoirs* 'an awful book', and records that it was published 'to almost universal scorn'. The portrait of her father was considered, says Harman, 'absurdly idealised, and the book did nothing but harm to the reputation Fanny had been so keen to foster.' His achievements were exaggerated, his character sweetened, for in reality he was a self-pitying, irascible, pushing man, tempered by his undoubted charm. Fanny stressed the latter quality to the point of untruthfulness, as in this Johnsonian sentence about Burney's life at Lynn: 'He scarcely ever entered a house upon terms of business without leaving it on terms of intimacy.' The book also contained an unpleasant note of self-abasement, as when Fanny calls herself 'the Recluse of West Humble' and 'Your unworthy humble servant', but at the same time she elevated her role in her father's life beyond her desserts and was not innocent of vanity, like her insinuation that she was much younger than 25 when *Evelina* was published. Throughout, one hears an echo of her admission that truth and fiction were sometimes 'indivisible' in her mind.

Her last years were not happy. In her eighties she was generally remembered for two books she had written in her twenties. One by one her remaining siblings died: James in 1821, Hetty in 1832, Charlotte in 1838. She became depressed, deaf and nearly blind. Her son's fiancée, Mary Ann Smith, moved in to keep her company, and friends like George Cambridge would call on her regularly out of duty and affection. She made her Will, signing it Frances d'Arblay, 'otherwise la Comtesse Veuve Piochard d'Arblay', leaving all her personal papers to her niece Charlotte Barrett, who published a selection of the diaries and letters in a seven-volume edition in the 1840s, which gave Fanny's fame a new dimension. As she weakened, Charlotte read St. John's Gospel to her, till Fanny said, 'My dear, I cannot understand a word – not a syllable!' On 6th January 1840 she died.

She was buried in Bath alongside her husband and son. Her heirs raised within St. Swithin's church a memorial as elaborate in its tributes as that which she had composed for her husband. It named her as Frances d'Arblay, and celebrated her as 'the friend of Johnson and of Burke, Who by her talents has obtained a name, Far more durable than marble can confer'. This eulogy, though it could not have been foreseen, was fully justified, for in 1957 the memorial disappeared, inexplicably, from the church and has not been seen since.

Fanny Burney's name suffered only intermittent eclipse, and in recent years it has shone again with the republication of all her novels, the performance of some of her plays, and the reading and constant quotation of her diaries and letters, which for her time were unequalled for their vivacity, interest and wit. Today the author of *Evelina* and *Cecilia*, which created new dimensions for the novel, is as well remembered for her memoirs of Johnson, the Court of George III, her mastectomy and the drama of the battle of Waterloo.

It is wholly fitting that in the year of this book's publication and the 250th anniversary of her birth, her name should be placed near her father's in the corner of Westminster Abbey dedicated to poets, writers and musicians of renown.

BIBLIOGRAPHY

This study makes no claim to original research. I have drawn upon Joyce Hemlow's twelve-volume edition of Fanny's diaries and letters, beginning in 1791, and her one-volume selection from them (1987), and the first four of a projected twelve-volume edition of the earlier years, 1768-90, edited under the direction of Professor Lars E. Troide. These, together with Fanny Burney's published novels and plays, and the *Memoir* of her father, are the basic tools of her recent biographers, among whom I am grateful to:

Margaret Ann Doody, *Fanny Burney, The Life in the Works* (1987)

Linda Kelly, *Juniper Hall* (1991)

Kate Chisholm, *Fanny Burney, Her Life* (1998)

Maggie Lane, *Bath through the eyes of Fanny Burney* (1999)

Claire Harman, *Fanny Burney, A Biography* (2000)

Hester Davenport, *Faithful Handmaid: Fanny Burney at the Court of King George III* (2000)

And I thank the librarian of the Berg Collection, New York Public Library, for allowing me to examine some of their Burney manuscripts.

In case of difficulty in purchasing any Short Books title
through normal channels, books can be purchased through
BOOKPOST:
Telephone – 01624 836000
Fax – 01624 837033
Email – bookshop@enterprise.net
www.bookpost.co.uk